AMAZING
ANIMALS Q&A

Written by David Burnie
Consultant Dr. Kim Dennis-Bryan

LONDON, NEW YORK, MELBOURNE, MUNICH, AND DELHI

Senior Art Editor Smiljka Surla
Senior Editor Fran Jones
Managing Editor Linda Esposito
Managing Art Editor Diane Thistlethwaite
Publishing Manager Andrew Macintyre
Category Publisher Laura Buller
Design Development Manager Sophia M. Tampakopoulos
Production Controller Georgina Hayworth
Picture Research Jo Walton
DK Picture Library Claire Bowers
DTP Designer Andy Hilliard
Jacket Editor Mariza O'Keefe
US Editor Margaret Parrish
Jacket Designers Johnny Pau, Rebecca Wright

DK Delhi
Designers Neerja Rawat, Tannishtha Chakraborty
Design Manager Kavita Dutta
Art Director Shefali Upadhyay

First published in the United States in 2007
by DK Publishing
375 Hudson Street
New York, New York 10014

Copyright © 2007 Dorling Kindersley Limited

07 08 09 10 11 10 9 8 7 6 5 4 3 2
AD360 – 05/07

A catalog record for this book is available from the Library of Congress.

ISBN 978-0-7566-2914-4

Color reproduction by Colorscan, Singapore
Printed and bound in China by Hung Hing

Discover more at
www.dk.com

CONTENTS

SENSES

Are eight eyes better than two?

For most animals, two eyes are all they need to find food and to keep out of harm's way. The position of these eyes is important, because it conrols how much the animal can see without moving its head. Spiders are different. They have up to eight eyes, looking forward and to either side. In jumping spiders, the two eyes that face forward are extra-large, helping them to judge distances when they leap on their unsuspecting prey. Despite having lots of eyes, most other spiders are nearsighted.

Q **Why do snails have eyes on stalks?**

A Snails need to see, but they also need to fit inside their shells. Having eyes on stalks lets them do both. Their eye-stalks are long and thin, which gives them a good view. But if a hungry bird lands near a snail, the eye-stalks shrink, like tiny telescopes folding up. This lets the snail disappear fully inside its shell.

Eye at the tip of each eye-stalk

Garden snail

Large, forward-pointing eyes

Knees flick suddenly when the spider jumps

Jumping spider

Front legs used for grabbing prey

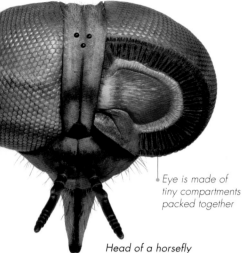

Eye is made of tiny compartments packed together

Head of a horsefly

Q A How do an insect's eyes work?

Insect eyes are very different from ours. They are hard instead of soft, and they are divided into hundreds or thousands of tiny compartments. Each compartment is like a mini-eye, and they work together to give the insect a view of its surroundings. Some insects—such as dragonflies and horseflies—have big, bulging eyes. They can see in every direction at once without having to move their heads.

Q A Who has the sharpest eyesight?

Birds of prey—such as kites and eagles—have smaller eyes than humans, but their eyesight is at least four times sharper. This means they are excellent at seeing small details, and at spotting food from high up in the air. Using its sharp eyesight, a kite can swoop down on a mouse or a young rabbit before its prey even knows that it is there.

Q A Who has the largest eyes of all?

These belong to the giant squid. This deep-sea animal can measure more than 23 ft (7 m) long with eyes up to 20 in (50 cm) across. Giant squid use their huge eyes to seek out fish and other animals in the murky depths of the sea.

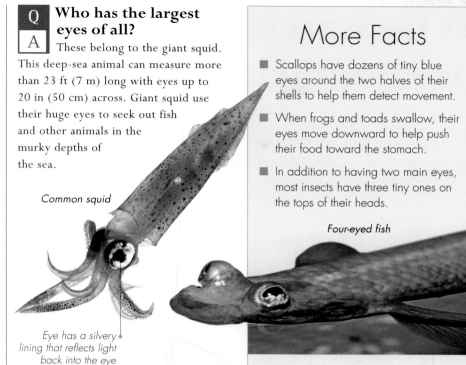

Common squid

Eye has a silvery lining that reflects light back into the eye

Q A Why do animals have wide-set eyes?

Grazing mammals, such as gazelles, have to stay on the lookout for danger in their grassland habitats. While their heads are down eating, there is always a chance that a predator will attack. Eyes that face sideways give an almost all-around view. Gazelles often feed in herds. They take turns looking up, making it harder for a predator to launch a surprise attack.

More Facts

- Scallops have dozens of tiny blue eyes around the two halves of their shells to help them detect movement.

- When frogs and toads swallow, their eyes move downward to help push their food toward the stomach.

- In addition to having two main eyes, most insects have three tiny ones on the tops of their heads.

Four-eyed fish

- The four-eyed fish lives in shallow water, and each of its eyes is divided in two. The bottom part looks downward into the water, while the top part looks upward into the air.

Thomson's gazelle

Forward-facing eyes shaded by feathery "eyebrows"

Red kite

Eyes on side of head give all-around vision

Who can see best in the dark?

Lots of animals move around at night and use their eyes to find the way. Owls have the best nighttime vision, allowing them to swerve and swoop safely between the trees. An owl's eyes are specially shaped for working well when the light is faint. Their pupils are extra-large so that as much light as possible can shine inside. But nighttime animals are not the only ones that live in the dark. Under the ground and in caves, there are creatures for whom it is dark all the time.

Pupils widen at night to let in the most light

Camouflaged feathers hide the owl during the day

Scops owl

Q A **Do earthworms have any eyes?**
No, they don't. Instead, they have tiny light sensors all over their bodies—mostly on their heads and tails. These sensors are too small to see things in any detail. They simply tell a worm how much light there is. If a worm is dug up, it uses its light sensors to crawl away from the light, back to safety underground.

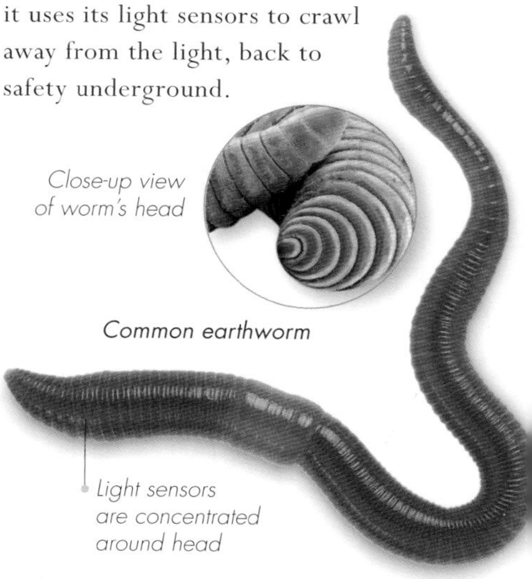

Close-up view of worm's head

Common earthworm

Light sensors are concentrated around head

Q A **How do cats' eyes change after dark?**
In bright sunshine, the pupils in a cat's eyes look like narrow slits. This shape stops the cat from being dazzled, because it prevents too much light getting in. After dark, the pupils widen until they are circular, letting far more light into the eyes. This change gives cats the best of both worlds. They can see well during the daytime and also after dark.

Pupils wide open in dim light

Domestic cat

Cat's pupils reduce to a slit when the light is bright

Moth

Moth attracted by lightbulb

Q A Why do moths fly toward light?

In nature, moths often use the Moon like a compass, to help them find their way. But if a moth flies near a house, bright lights can upset its navigation system. Instead of flying past the light, the moth keeps turning toward it, until it ends up spiraling around it, or fluttering at a window. Moths can't help doing this, and fly away if the light is switched off.

More Facts

- Owls cannot move their eyes in their sockets, so they have to turn their heads to look around them.

- Some lizards have such long tongues that they can use them to wipe their eyes.

- Snakes do not have any eyelids, so they cannot blink. Their eyes stay wide open even when they are asleep.

- The blind cave fish, from Central America, does not have any eyes. It finds its way by sensing faint waves of pressure in the water around it.

Blind cave fish

Lesser bushbaby

Large, round eyes to see in the dark

Q A Who takes a leap in the dark?

Bushbabies are amazingly agile, even though they only move around at night. They live in trees and often leap through the darkness as they scamper from branch to branch. They can do this because their eyes have a special layer at the back, which works like a mirror. It reflects light back into their eyes, giving them a brighter view. Many nocturnal mammals share this way of seeing in the dark.

Pink tentacles on nose

Star-nosed mole

Q A Which animal "sees" with its nose?

The star-nosed mole has tiny eyes, and is almost totally blind. But at the end of its nose, it has a circle of 22 bright pink fleshy tentacles. These tentacles can move, and they work like tiny fingers. The mole uses them to find its way, and—even more importantly—to find its food. These moles spend most of their lives in burrows, where "seeing" with tentacles is more useful than seeing with eyes.

Q A What helps a snake to see in the dark?

Rattlesnakes and their relatives are specially equipped for hunting after dark. In front of their eyes, they have a pair of special hollows, or pits. These pits contain hundreds of tiny sensors, which can detect heat. If the snake comes close to a warm-blooded animal—such as a mouse or a hare—it can detect its prey by the heat that it gives off.

Eyes with slit-shaped pupils

Pit viper

Heat-sensitive pit between eye and nostril

Are big ears helpful?

Hearing is important for lots of animals, but mammals are the only ones with ears that have fleshy lobes. An African elephant's ears are by far the largest. They can be 6 ft (1.8 m) high and more than 3 ft (1 m) wide. The ears are highly sensitive, and can pick up sounds from other elephants that are pitched too low for humans to hear. Elephants also use their ears to keep cool, and they spread them wide if they are alarmed or angry. But ears don't have to be big to work well. Lots of animals with less obvious ears—or ears that are hidden—can hear better than humans.

Q A How do bats find food with their ears?

Long-eared bats hunt insects after dark. Instead of looking for insects, they find them by making high-pitched clicks as they flit through the air. If an insect is in range, the bat hears the echoes that bounce back, and uses them to guide it toward its prey. This way of steering is called echolocation. Most insect-eating bats track down food in this way.

Elephants keep cool by slowly flapping their ears

Large ears act like funnels to collect sound

Fox can also swivel its ears to listen for danger

Fennec fox

Q A Which mammal has the best hearing?

Elephants are good at hearing low-pitched sounds, but the tiny fennec fox is much better at hearing sounds that are faint or high-pitched. The fox lives in the Sahara Desert, where it comes out at night to feed on insects and lizards. Its outsize ears can pick up the sound of a single beetle as it scurries across the ground. They also help the fox to keep cool by giving off body heat.

Extra-large ears pick up echoes from insect prey

Snout helps to focus the bat's clicks

Brown long-eared bat

Ear shape is unique, like a human fingerprint

Q A Which insect has ears near its knees?

Unlike mammals, insects don't always have ears on their heads. Crickets have an ear on each front leg, just below the knee. The ear does not have a flap—instead, it is a small oval slit. Hearing is important to crickets because the males "sing" to attract a mate. Grasshoppers sing as well, but their ears are on the sides of their bodies, just beneath their wings.

Close-up view of ear on front leg

Female bush cricket

Mexican milksnake

Q A Is it true that snakes are deaf?

Unlike lizards, snakes do not have ears, but even so, they are not completely deaf. Scientists are not sure exactly how they hear, but they probably "feel" sound waves with their bodies and with sensors inside their heads. Snakes are known to be very good at feeling vibrations in the ground. If they sense footsteps heading toward them, most of them quickly slither away.

Q A Do frogs and toads have ears?

Yes—if you look closely at a frog or a toad, its ears are often easy to see. Instead of sticking out, each one is like a circular patch, just behind the eyes. This patch is an eardrum, and it vibrates when it picks up sound. Frogs and toads can be noisy animals, particularly at breeding time. They use their ears to listen for each other's calls, so that they can find a mate.

Female African elephant

More Facts

Dolphin hunting fish

■ Dolphins use echolocation to find food, and to steer clear of the seabed after dark.

■ Rhinoceros ears swivel around, allowing them to hear sounds from almost any direction.

■ Although giraffes were thought to be mute, scientists now believe that they communicate with each other at a level too low to be heard by humans.

Eardrum on surface of body

American bullfrog

Do birds have noses?

Most animals have a sense of smell, but their noses—or nostrils—are not always where you might expect them to be. Birds usually have their noses on top of their beaks, or sometimes even inside them. Albatrosses have extra-large noses and a great sense of smell. This helps them to sniff out food floating on the sea, even after dark. Not many birds' noses are as sensitive as this, and some can hardly smell at all. However, for most animals, a keen sense of smell is vital for survival.

Mother sheep recognizes her lamb's distinctive smell

Female sheep and lambs

Albatross

Long tube-shaped nostrils on top of beak

Q A Why do sheep smell their lambs?

Female sheep (ewes) generally have one to three lambs per birth. After a sheep has given birth, she licks her lambs all over and gets to know their smell. This is very important, because she uses smell to identify which lambs are hers. If another sheep's lamb comes close and tries to drink her milk, she will push it away. Many other mammals, from mice to antelopes, use their noses in the same way, to tell who is who.

Large, hooked beak for grabbing slippery fish

Rhinoceros and calf

Rhino dung

Q A What do rhinos do with their dung?

Some animals bury their dung, but rhinoceroses do just the opposite—they put it on display. They leave their dung in piles, which can measure more than 3 ft (1 m) across. A large male can have up to 30 piles, which he visits almost every day. Rhinos use these dung piles to mark the edges of their territory. It works well, because they have poor eyesight, but an excellent sense of smell.

Q/A Who has the keenest sense of smell?

Male moths break all records with their sense of smell. Their feathery antennae work like noses, because they collect particles of scent given off by female moths as they flutter through the air. Some males are so good at this that they can sense a single female moth more than 6 miles (10 km) away. At this distance, the scent is millions of times too faint for a human nose to detect.

Males have feathery antennae— the best shape for collecting scent

Male moth

Bloodhound

More Facts

- Monitor lizards smell in the same way as snakes, by flicking out their tongues. The biggest monitor—the Komodo dragon—has a tongue that can be 12 in (30 cm) long.

- The kiwi is the only bird with nostrils at the end of its beak. It probes damp soil after dark, sniffing out earthworms and insects.

- Sharks use smell to track down prey. Those that live in open water can smell blood from miles away. Bottom-feeders, like the Port Jackson shark, smell animals hiding on the seabed.

Port Jackson shark

Q/A Why do snakes flick out their tongues?

Instead of smelling with their noses, snakes use their tongues. A snake collects particles of airborne scent on its tongue and then presses them into special hollows in the roof of the mouth. Nerves in the hollows detect the scent in the same way as a nose. If a snake keeps flicking its tongue rapidly, it is a sign that something interesting is in the air.

Forked tongue collects scent particles from the air

Q/A Who is the best animal detective?

All dogs have a good sense of smell, but a bloodhound's is more than 10 million times better than a human's. These dogs can detect the smell of a person's skin cells even if they are several days old, and they can stay on the right trail even if the person has walked through crowded places, such as shopping malls. Smells are identified by scent receptors in the dog's nasal chambers, and the bloodhound has extra-large chambers. Bloodhounds can be used to help solve crimes.

Red-tailed rat snake

Who loves a sugary drink?

Taste tells animals what is good to eat—and what might be unpleasant. For hummingbirds, tasty food is always sweet. Like bees, hummingbirds feed on nectar, a sugary juice made by flowers. Their beaks are shaped like drinking straws, and their tongues lap up the nectar while they hover in the air. Not all animals taste with their tongues—some insects taste with their feet. Other animals rely on touch to find their food.

Wings beat up to 80 times a second—faster than any other bird

Nectar in base of flower

Beak stays steady while the hummingbird feeds

Rufous-tailed hummingbird

Giant anteater

Tongue flicks in and out about 150 times a minute

Which animal has the longest tongue?
The giant anteater has one of the longest tongues. It can be 2 ft (60 cm) long, and is covered in sticky saliva and small spines to extract prey from nests and mounds. The anteater flicks its tongue deep into ants' nests, collecting up to 30,000 ants a day. Although it has no teeth, the anteater swallows pebbles to crush ants in its stomach.

Can flies taste with their feet?
Yes, they can—and so can some other insects, such as butterflies. This way of tasting is a great time-saver, because it tells insects if they are on food as soon as they land. Houseflies use their feet like this whenever they settle indoors. If they taste something sweet, they mop it up with their tongues, which work like sponges.

Housefly

Fly's tongue folds away after use

Which animal has the longest feelers?

Q **A** If a lobster survives to a ripe old age, its feelers—or antennae—can be over 3 ft (1 m) long. These feelers can taste as well as touch, and the lobster uses them to find food in the dark. A lobster's feelers grow each time that it sheds its skin. They also grow back if they are lost in accidents, although it takes them time to reach their full size.

Lobsters have two pairs of feelers—one long pair and one short pair

Lobster

Walrus

Whiskers used for finding food on the seabed

Tusks can be used to haul walrus out of the water onto the ice

Who is the world's touchiest animal?

Q **A** Naked mole rats live underground and have very limited vision. Instead, they rely on their amazing sense of touch. Their skin is practically hairless, but they do have several dozen whiskerlike hairs on each side of their bodies. If just one of these hairs is touched, a mole rat turns around to find out what made it move. Naked mole rats live in family groups, and they feed on plant roots, gnawing them with their sharp front teeth.

Whiskers and bristles used for feeling the way underground

Why do walruses have bristly whiskers?

Q **A** Unlike seals, walruses dive down to the seabed to eat. They swallow lots of small animals, but they particularly like worms, sea cucumbers, and clams. Where walruses feed, the seabed is often murky, and this is where whiskers are useful. Instead of looking for a meal, walruses feel with their whiskers. When they touch food, they use their mouths like a vacuum cleaner to suck up their prey.

More Facts

- Some of the world's smallest moths have feelers that are four times as long as their bodies.

- European jewel beetles sense the heat from forest fires. They fly toward the heat to lay their eggs on warm tree bark.

- If threatened, a porcupine will back into its enemy, piercing the animal's flesh with its barbed quills.

- Cabbage white caterpillars are attracted to the peppery taste of cabbage leaves.

- Bird-eating spiders use touch to feel for food when they hunt after dark.

- Anchored to rocks in shallow water, a sea anemone waits for small creatures to touch its tentacles. It then attacks with hundreds of tiny stings.

Sea anemone

Naked mole rats

FIGHT OR FLIGHT

Who is the largest land predator?

When it comes to hunting, size often helps. Among the big killers are brown bears, or grizzlies—by far the largest hunters on land. Brown bears can stand 11 ft 2 in (3.4 m) tall, have massive teeth and claws, and are incredibly strong. Although they usually shuffle along at a steady pace, they can move quickly in pursuit of prey. Fortunately, brown bears usually keep clear of people. Size isn't always important to a predator—sometimes small can be just as deadly.

Venom sac

Rear end of honeybee

Barbed, needlelike stinger

Q A **Are bees ever deadly?**
Yes, they can be. Bees only sting as a defense mechanism, and whether it proves deadly depends on the location of the sting. If the bee stings an animal's mouth or throat, for example, the danger is greater. For most people, a bee sting hurts as venom is pumped into the body, but the pain goes away. But if someone is allergic to bee stings, their body starts to react. They may find it hard to breathe, and without help, they may die.

Brown bears

Teeth for eating meat or plant food

Strong, powerfully built body

Q A How does a jellyfish kill its prey?
Sea wasps, a type of jellyfish, carry a potent venom in their tentacles. Any small fish brushing against a section of tentacle will probably die. Jellyfish need to kill their prey quickly because they have no way of holding onto them so they cannot swim away. Sea wasps live off the north coast of Australia, and can be a danger to people who swim there.

Venom is injected by teeth in lower jaw

Fat is stored in the tail as a food reserve for periods of drought

Sharp claws used to dig burrows

Gila monster

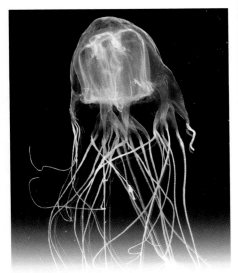

Sea wasp (box jellyfish)

Q A Which snake has the strongest venom?
The hook-nosed sea-snake, from the Indian Ocean, is by far the most venomous snake in the world. On land, the inland taipan from Australia tops the venom list. It contains enough venom to kill about 100 people, but because it is shy, it rarely causes problems.

Q A Are lizards ever poisonous?
Until recently, only two lizards were known to be poisonous—the gila monster and the beaded lizard. These fat-bodied lizards live in the deserts of North America. They attack small animals and hold on when they bite, giving their venom time to work. Scientists have recently discovered that some monitor lizards are also poisonous.

More Facts

- A hippo will attack if it is threatened. It can bite a small boat in two with its powerful jaws and enormous teeth.

- The Brazilian wandering spider has such powerful venom that it can kill people with a single bite.

- The tsetse fly, from Africa, is one of the world's most dangerous insects. It sucks blood to feed, often spreading a fatal disease called sleeping sickness.

Q A Who is the biggest hunter in the world?
Measuring up to 67 ft (20 m) long, sperm whales are the largest predators. They dive down to the sea's dark depths, where they hunt giant squid. Unlike other big whales, sperm whales have teeth for killing their prey, which they track down by using sound.

Snake can be 8 ft (2.5 m) long

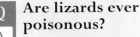

Inland taipan

Body is covered with small light-brown scales

Sperm whale

Tsetse fly

Large eyes

Which animal packs a mighty punch?

During the breeding season, male animals often fight to decide who gets a chance to mate. Some use their antlers or horns as weapons, while others kick or bite. Male kangaroos use a different technique—they stand up on their hind legs and box with their front paws. Each male tries to push the other off balance, and the contest continues until one ends up on the ground. Animal fights may look scary, but it's rare for contestants to get hurt. Once the winner has triumphed, the fight stops and the loser makes a getaway. With experience, he may be luckier next time.

More Facts

- Rattlesnakes fight by twining around each other. They keep their mouths shut, so there is no risk of being bitten.

- In the Arctic, musk oxen fight by running toward each other at full speed, so that they crash head-on with their horns.

- Fights between elephant seals can be extremely fierce. The seals bite each other on the head and neck, and often end up covered with blood.

- Scorpions fight by locking their pincers together. This keeps them out of range of each other's sting.

Scorpions

Head tipped back to avoid opponent's punches

Gray kangaroos

Front legs used for punching and grappling

Great egrets

Wings raised up during fight

Q/A How did fighting fish get their name?

Wild fighting fish live in ponds and streams in Southeast Asia. The females are peaceful, but the males attack each other on sight, biting each other and lashing out with their tails. They are not much longer than a finger, but they make themselves look bigger by opening up their fins. Fighting fish are popular as pets, but because they are aggressive, only one male can be kept in each tank.

Siamese fighting fish

Fins opened out to look large

The bigger the swing, the harder the blow

Giraffes

Q/A What is a bird's best weapon?

Birds don't have teeth, so they cannot bite each other when they fight. Instead, they often use their beaks. An egret's beak can be more than 10 in (25 cm) long, and has a deadly point that it uses to stab right through a fish. But when egrets fight, they do not do too much harm. Instead of stabbing at each other, they keep their beaks open and peck at their opponent's neck and wings.

Q/A Who uses its head to butt in a fight?

Instead of fighting with their feet, giraffes use their necks and heads. A giraffe braces itself by stiffening its legs, then swinging its head over its shoulders, toward its rival's neck. Often the blow misses, but just occasionally, it hits so hard that the other giraffe may be knocked out.

Every zebra has a different stripe pattern

Plains zebras

Q/A Why do male deer have antlers?

During the breeding season, male deer use their antlers in tests of strength. Rivals face each other, and then rush forward until their antlers are locked together. They push as hard as they can, until one forces the other backward, and away from the battleground. Once this happens, the loser pulls its antlers free and runs away.

Q/A Can zebras hurt with their hooves?

When zebras fight, they often nip each other with their large teeth. But when disputes get serious, they swing around and kick out with their back feet. A well-aimed kick hits the opponent in the chest or the ribs, giving it a painful bruise. If zebras are cornered by a predator and cannot run away, they use the same technique. Some zebras also make loud braying noises during a fight.

Males grow a new pair of antlers each year

Male deer

How does a hunter make a kill?

In the animal world, hunters work in many different ways to catch prey. Some, like the cheetah, rely on speed and strength to make a kill. Others, such as the praying mantis, play a game of patience. A mantis will stay still for hours at a time, watching for any insects that come nearby. If a fly lands within range, the mantis reacts instantly and grabs the fly with its front legs. It starts to eat right away—even if the fly is still struggling. Other animals have more cunning methods of luring prey into their hungry mouths.

Tawny eagle

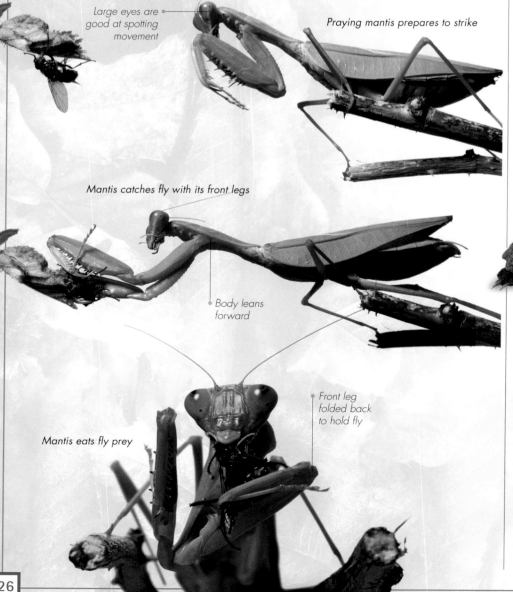

Large eyes are good at spotting movement

Praying mantis prepares to strike

Mantis catches fly with its front legs

Body leans forward

Mantis eats fly prey

Front leg folded back to hold fly

Q A Who is the world's craftiest reptile?

The alligator snapping turtle lurks at the bottom of lakes with its mouth wide open. Its tongue is pink and wriggles just like a worm so that it makes a tempting sight to passing fish. But if a fish comes close, the turtle snaps shut its powerful jaws, often chopping the fish in half. These turtles can be identified by the three large ridges that run vertically down their shells.

Snapping turtle

Pink tongue attracts fish

Q A What is a cheetah's secret weapon?

The answer is simple—speed. Cheetahs are the world's fastest land animals and, over a short distance, they can hit 60 mph (100 km/h). They can do this because they have a huge stride, thanks to their long legs and their very flexible spine. They also have special claws that give extra grip on the ground—just like an athlete's shoes.

Cheetah

Wide-open wings work like brakes

Sharp eyesight

Hooked beak to rip prey apart

Powerful toes with sharp claws

Unsuspecting insect is a sitting target

Fish directs jet of water up toward insect

Archer fish

More Facts

■ Electric eels kill fish by giving them a 600-volt electric shock. The eel's muscles work like batteries, storing up an electric charge.

■ Instead of making webs, bolas spiders catch flying insects with a single strand of silk. They tip the strand with a blob of glue, and then swing it in the air.

■ Scorpions use their stings for self-defense, but they tear their prey apart with their claws.

■ Cone shells are beautiful but deadly. They attack fish with poisonous mouthparts that work like harpoons. They have also killed people who picked them up on beaches at low tide.

Cone shell

Q A Which fish shoots down its prey?

Lots of fish leap after insects, but the archer fish is the only one that shoots them down. It looks for insects on waterside plants, and then takes careful aim. By squeezing its mouth, it squirts a jet of water toward the insect, knocking it off balance and into its waiting jaws.

Poison claws

Giant centipede

Q A Which hunter has poisonous claws?

Centipedes hunt after dark, and attack their prey with two poison claws, which are positioned just behind their heads. Most centipedes hunt insects and other small animals, but the giant centipede can kill frogs and mice. It has bright red and black markings, and can be up to 12 in (30 cm) long.

Q A How do eagles grab their prey?

Birds of prey—such as eagles and hawks—do not hunt with their beaks. Instead, they stab animals with their talons, or extra-sharp claws. Once they have made a kill, they carry the animal back to a perch, where they use their hooked beaks to rip it apart. The smallest birds of prey hunt insects, but the biggest ones can snatch monkeys out of trees.

Why do skunks kick up a stink?

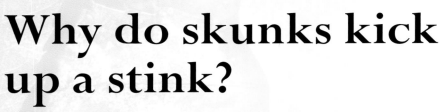

With so many hunters on the prowl, most animals need ways to get out of trouble. Lots of them escape as fast as they can, using their legs, wings, or fins. Skunks do not always take flight. If anything threatens them, they arch their backs and lift their tails to look threatening. If that doesn't work, they squirt a horrible-smelling fluid from the base of their tails. The stink lasts for days, and the fluid can cause blindness if it hits an animal's eyes.

Two white stripes run from head to tail and meet again at the base of the tail

 Q A Which reptile can run across water?

If a basilisk lizard is being chased, it heads for the nearest river or stream. Using its extra-large back legs, it runs across the surface of the water. Flaps of skin between each toe provide extra surface area on the water. Basilisks cannot run far before they start to sink, but this extraordinary escape trick is often enough to save their skins.

Raised tail shows that the skunk is ready to fight back

Striped skunk

Basilisk lizard

Long, powerful hind legs

Brown hare

Q A Which animal is quickest off the mark?

Hares have only one way of protecting themselves—they run as fast as they can. They have extremely good eyesight, which means that they can start running when a predator is still a long way off. Instead of running in a straight line, hares zigzag their way across open countryside. This unusual technique makes it even harder for another animal to catch them.

Octopus

Q A What disappears in a cloud of ink?

Octopuses do. They eject a liquid that looks like ink. The octopus mixes the ink with water, and then squirts it out in a powerful jet. The force of the jet pushes the octopus backward, and out of harm's way. Meanwhile, the predator is engulfed by the inky cloud.

Q A Who can dig its way to safety?

Lots of animals make burrows, but few of them can beat the aardvark at high-speed digging. If it is being pursued, this piglike mammal starts digging furiously with its powerful front claws. If the ground is soft, the animal soon starts to disappear to safety below the surface. When threatened, the aardvark may roll on its back and defend itself with its claws.

Long ears are held upright but can be folded down

Aardvark

Who rolls up in a ball?

Instead of running away from trouble, the pill millipede rolls up into a ball. It is protected by its hard body case, and its head and legs are safely tucked up inside. It stays like this until all seems to be quiet outside. Other animals that do this include hedgehogs, woodlice, and three-banded armadillos, which turn themselves into solid balls covered with rows of bony plates.

1 The millipede has a jointed body case that allows it to curl up into a tight ball when facing danger.

2 It tucks away its fragile body parts as it curls into a tight and inpenetrable ball.

3 Once danger has passed, the millipede can start to unroll itself and move safely on its way.

Flying fish

Q A Which fish can glide through the air?

There is nowhere to hide from danger near the surface of the sea. For flying fish, this is not a problem. If something chases them, they burst upward through the surface, and then glide through the air on their outstretched fins. Some flying fish trail their tails in the water and use them like propellers. They speed through the air for up to 1,300 ft (400 m), leaving any predator behind.

Head stays very steady while the bird runs

Q A Who runs fastest on two legs?

A flightless bird, the ostrich, is the fastest biped. If an ostrich is cornered, it can defend itself with a powerful kick. But in the open, ostriches usually react to danger by running away. An ostrich's feet are like hooves, with just two toes, and its long, elastic leg muscles give it a top speed of more than 45 mph (70 km/h). Even ostrich chicks, a few days old, can run pretty fast.

Ostrich

Wings held close to body

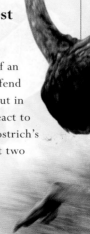

CAMOUFLAGE AND COLOR

Why do tigers have stripes?

Lots of animals have patterns and colors that make them difficult to see. Most use their camouflage to hide from predators, but some predators—such as tigers—also need camouflage themselves. Tigers hunt by stealth, and their stripes help to break up their outline as they slink through tropical forests or waist-high grass. This lets them get close to their prey, so they can launch a sudden and deadly attack.

Bengal tiger

Tawny frogmouth

Q A Which bird looks like a piece of wood?

The tawny frogmouth, from Australia, is one of the world's best camouflaged birds. It hunts small animals after dark, but spends the day asleep in trees. During the day, it is almost impossible to see. It perches bolt upright, and its gray feathers make it look like a broken branch. It keeps perfectly still so that it does not give itself away.

Gaboon viper

Fallen leaves camouflage the snake

Q A Who behaves like a snake in the grass?

The Gaboon viper is armed with deadly fangs. Out in the open, its intricate markings make it easy to see. When it lies among fallen leaves, however, its camouflage makes it disappear. Gaboon vipers hunt by watching and waiting on the forest floor. If suitable prey comes within range, they immediately strike. This viper has venom powerful enough to kill people.

Which is the weirdest animal disguise?

Q A It's hard to imagine anyone wanting to eat a bird dropping. That's why some spiders and caterpillars use bird droppings as a disguise. They have gray and white bodies, and sit out on leaves— exactly where a bird dropping might land. To make their disguise convincing, they form a shape like a blob. Spiders pull in their legs, while caterpillars curl up.

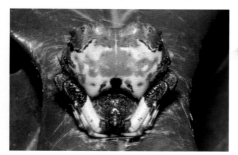

Bird-dropping spider

What looks like seaweed on the move?

Q A Many fish use camouflage, but the leafy seadragon has a clever disguise. Its body is covered with leaflike flaps, making it look like a piece of drifting weed. It swims with its body upright, but its tiny fins make it one of the slowest fish. These seadragons live off the coast of southern Australia, close to seaweed-covered rocks. If a seadragon is washed up on shore, its leafy flaps soon collapse.

Leafy seadragon

Leaf-tailed gecko

The lizard even has camouflaged eyes

When does a butterfly look like a leaf?

Dead leaves often lie on the ground, so we hardly ever give them a second look. But in some places, they are not what they seem. The Indian leaf butterfly, from southern Asia, mimics dead leaves to keep from being seen. Lots of other insects, including moths and leaf insects, use the same kind of disguise.

1 This Indian leaf butterfly is resting among some dead leaves. Its beautifully camouflaged wings make it almost impossible to see.

2 This is the same butterfly, seen from below, with its wings open. Its hindwings each have a tail that looks just like a leaf stalk.

3 From above, the butterfly looks very different. These bright colors are only visible when the butterfly is in the air.

Which lizard plays hide and seek?

Q A The leaf-tailed gecko is expert at hiding against the bark of a tree. Compared to most lizards, it has a flat body. It also has a tail like a dried-out leaf and gray skin with markings like cracks in wood. These geckos hunt insects at night. If a predator does spot it, the lizard can quickly shed its tail— a trick that confuses the enemy while it escapes. A new tail slowly grows back.

Which insects disguise themselves as thorns?

Q A Lined up on a twig, treehoppers are not easy to see. They have a special trick for survival—they look exactly like thorns. Behind their heads they have a hard shield, which stretches up in a thorn-shaped spike. Treehoppers use their camouflage to protect themselves from hungry birds.

Green and brown coloring helps them merge with the tree

Treehoppers

Who has the most colorful face?

The animal world is full of bright colors, specially in warm parts of the world. Brilliantly colored fish swim among coral reefs, and colorful insects and frogs live in tropical forests. Color helps animals to recognize their own kind, and to tell males and females apart. Mammals often have camouflage colors, but one monkey— the male mandrill—really stands out. The bare skin on its muzzle looks as if it were covered with red and blue paint.

Curved claws hook onto branches

Three-toed sloth

Male mandrill

Olive-gray fur

More Facts

- Many birds and insects can see colors that are invisible to humans. This is because their eyes can detect ultraviolet light.

- The forceps fish changes its colors and its pattern as it grows up. The young and adult fish look as if they belong to two different species.

Adult forceps fish

Young forceps fish

- Humpback whales have individual black and white markings—each as different as a human fingerprint.

- Brown is the most common color in animals, while gold is one of the rarest.

Tiny organisms turn fur green

Baby clings to its mother's fur for six months

What makes sloths turn green?

Sloths feed on leaves and spend their lives hanging upside down from the branches of trees. When they are newborns, they have yellowish-brown fur, but they turn green as they grow. This color comes from tiny organisms, called algae. The algae grow on the sloth's fur, giving it a greenish tinge and a musty smell. The green color helps to hide sloths from eagles, which often search for prey in the treetops. Strangely, the algae also make a useful snack. They are full of nutrients sloths can lick off.

Arctic fox

Why do Arctic foxes go pale in winter?

In the Arctic, a brown fox would be easy to spot in winter as it would stand out against the snow. That's why Arctic foxes change color with the seasons. During the summer, most Arctic foxes are grayish-brown—a color that hides them among grass and rocks. When the summer is over, they grow a white winter coat, which has much thicker and warmer fur.

Color spots scattered across body

Tentacles with suckers

Who can change color in a second?

Some animals change their colors and patterns to match their background or to show their mood. A cuttlefish can do this in less than a second, thanks to special color spots just beneath its skin. As it swims over the seabed, it can make itself blend in with pebbles, seaweed, or sand. The cuttlefish may also change color to show fear or to startle a predator.

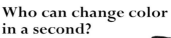

Cuttlefish (seen from below)

Each kind of frog has a different color and pattern

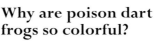

Leaf beetle

Shiny colors produced by body case

Why are poison dart frogs so colorful?

Many frogs have camouflage colors, but poison dart frogs are exactly the opposite. These tiny frogs live in Central and South America and are easy to see as they hop over the forest floor. They don't worry about being eaten, because their bodies contain a deadly poison. The bright colors work as a warning sign, showing other animals that they are too dangerous to touch. Forest people once used their poison to tip blowpipe darts.

Brilliant colors show up on the forest floor

Poison dart frogs

Body usually less than 2 in (5 cm) long

How do leaf beetles get their shine?

These shiny colors are made in a special way. Instead of being produced by chemicals, they are made by microscopic ridges on the beetle's body case. These ridges make light rays interfere with each other, creating colors with a metallic shine. Many other animals—including hummingbirds and butterflies—have shiny colors, which are made in a similar way.

Which lizard is the best actor?

The natural world is full of animal actors. Some pretend to be poisonous snakes or stinging insects, while others have frightening "eyes" to scare off attackers. All these animals act for the same reason—to make themselves look much more dangerous than they really are. The best dramatic actor is the frilled lizard from northern Australia. When cornered, it opens up a flap of skin that looks like an enormous scaly umbrella. At the same time, it hisses and lashes its tail from side to side. The frilled lizard can bite, but this eye-popping display often stops an attacker in its tracks, giving the lizard time to run for safety up a tree.

Q / A Who does a good imitation of a snake?

Most animals are frightened of snakes, even if they have never seen one. An elephant hawkmoth caterpillar uses this fear to protect itself. It has bright spots on the back of its head, which look like a pair of eyes. If the caterpillars are threatened by a bird, they pull in their heads and then hunch up into a snakelike shape. It's a trick that can save a caterpillar's life.

Elephant hawkmoth caterpillar

Q / A Which frog appears to have eyes on its back?

Normally, it's a bad idea to turn your back on danger. But the Chilean four-eyed frog does exactly that. It has a pair of swellings on its sides that look exactly like scary eyes. They lie just above the frog's legs and seem to turn its back into a large and threatening head. These false eyes are actually poison glands. If something does bite the frog, their horrible taste often makes it let go.

Mouth gapes open

Frilled lizard

Real eyes

Chilean four-eyed frog

Tail lashes from side to side

Feet have strong claws

Caterpillar's boldly marked eyespots

Real head tucked away out of sight

Virginia opossum

Frill of skin surrounds the lizard's neck

Narrow waist

Sting in tail

Common wasp

Q A Do animals ever play dead?

Yes, they do—and it sometimes saves their lives. One of the greatest experts is the Virginia opossum, a marsupial from North America. If it is cornered by a predator, it curls up with its eyes half-open, just as if it has died of fright. Many predators hunt only living animals, so if the opossum plays dead, its enemy will lose interest and move on. When the coast is clear, the opossum miraculously "comes back to life."

Tail with no sting

Thick waist

Clearwing moth

Q A Why do some moths look like wasps?

For moths, looking like a wasp is a great way of keeping out of trouble. Dressed up in black and yellow stripes, and with two pairs of see-through wings, they look almost like the real thing. Birds—and most humans too—are fooled into thinking that they can sting. Copying wasps is a very common trick in the animal world. Thousands of species of small animals, including flies and spiders, use it as a way to stay safe.

Q A Why do some birds pretend to be hurt?

A female plover nests on the ground—often a vulnerable place to be. If she sees an animal heading toward her eggs, the plover will try to lure it away. She leaves the nest and limps across the ground, pretending to drag a broken wing. With luck, the intruder follows her, hoping to catch an easy meal. When it seems safe, the plover "recovers" and flies back to her nest.

Female plover

More Facts

- Some spiders look like ants and move in the same jerky way. Ants can bite and sting, so birds and lizards are tricked into leaving them alone.

- The devil's coach horse beetle pretends to have a sting. It curls up its tail just like a scorpion.

- Hairstreak butterflies may have false heads on their hindwings. The false head draws birds away from the real head.

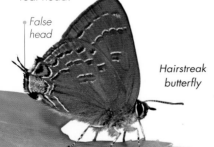

False head

Hairstreak butterfly

Who uses color to attract a mate?

To avoid danger, animals often do their best to keep out of sight. During the breeding season, however, they need to draw attention to themselves so they can attract a mate. Some animals do this by calling or singing or even changing color, but a male fiddler crab waves one giant, colored claw. This claw is as long as the fiddler crab's body. When the male waves, female crabs come scuttling across the mud. Claw-waving can also challenge other males to a fight.

Eyes on stalks help the crab to see across coastal mud

Small claw is used for picking food from the mud

Signaling claw is brightly colored, and too big to use for feeding

Male fiddler crab

Q A What makes a salmon blush?

At sea, sockeye salmon have silvery sides and steel-blue heads. Just before the breeding season, their bodies turn bright red. Millions of sockeyes then head for the coast before swimming up rivers to lakes, where they lay their eggs. The colors act as a signal, showing which adult fish are ready to breed.

Red breeding color

Sockeye salmon

Satin bowerbirds

Who is attracted by the color blue?

Q / **A** Male bowerbirds have amazing building skills. To attract females, each male collects hundreds of small sticks and makes a structure called a bower. The male then decorates the bower with bright objects and waits for his work to catch a female's eye. Satin bowerbirds, from Australia, always use blue in their color scheme. The males collect blue flowers, blue feathers, and even blue bottle caps to spread out on the ground.

Why do glow worms glow?

Q / **A** Glow worms are actually female beetles without wings. During the breeding season, they need to attract males, which fly around after dark. To do this, a glow worm curls her tail upward and switches on special panels that give off an eerie yellowish light. A male will land beside her to mate.

Glow worm climbs up grass after dark

Female glow worm

Who has good cheekbones?

Q / **A** In the world of humans, rugged features often make a handsome face. But female orangutans have different ideas about good looks. They prefer their partners to have extra-wide cheek pads, a fat pouch under their throats, and lots of long straggly fur. These features are found only in males, and they get more noticeable with age. Orangutans spend most of their lives alone, so females do not have a long time to choose a mate. A male's cheek pads show that he is mature and healthy, and will probably father strong and healthy young.

Male orangutan

More Facts

◼ Anolis lizards attract females by lowering a throat flap, which looks like a brightly colored flag.

Anolis lizard

Throat flap is also used to threaten enemies

◼ Male cracker butterflies make a snapping sound when they fly. The sound attracts females, but keeps other males away.

◼ Female fireflies produce light to attract males. Some attract other species, then eat them.

◼ A flightless bird, the great bustard, attracts females by fluffing up its feathers. At the height of its performance, the bird looks as if it has turned itself inside out.

Which bird gives a puffed-up performance?

Q / **A** Male and female frigate birds look almost identical as they circle high above the sea. But during the breeding season, the males have a startling way of catching a female's eye. Perched in a bush near the water's edge, they puff up a throat pouch that looks like a bright red balloon. Each male keeps his pouch inflated until he has successfully attracted a mate.

Hooked beak for catching fish

Male frigate bird

Pouch turns from orange to deep red during breeding season

EXTREME LIVING

How do termites avoid the heat?

For all animals—big or small—getting too warm can be deadly. That's why animals in hot places need ways of keeping cool. Some of them hide from the midday sun, or only come out after dark. Grassland termites beat the heat by living in air-conditioned nests. The part they live in is buried below the ground. Above them is a gigantic mound, made of sunbaked clay. Up to 13 ft (4 m) high, the mound contains tunnels that cool the air that circulates through the nest.

Termite

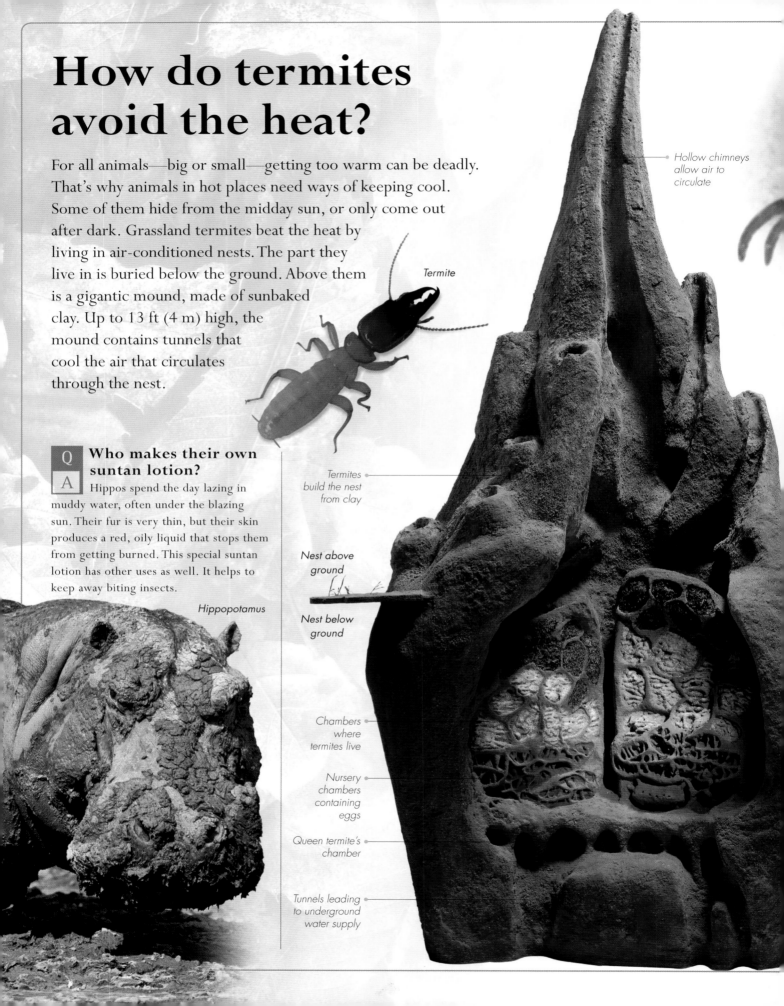

Hollow chimneys allow air to circulate

Termites build the nest from clay

Nest above ground

Nest below ground

Chambers where termites live

Nursery chambers containing eggs

Queen termite's chamber

Tunnels leading to underground water supply

Q / A Who makes their own suntan lotion?

Hippos spend the day lazing in muddy water, often under the blazing sun. Their fur is very thin, but their skin produces a red, oily liquid that stops them from getting burned. This special suntan lotion has other uses as well. It helps to keep away biting insects.

Hippopotamus

Foot raised to cool down

Shovel-snouted lizard

Q A Why do tarantulas hunt at night?

Unlike many spiders, tarantulas move slowly and feel their way toward their prey. In bright sunshine, a tarantula would be easy for predators to spot. Instead, tarantulas spend the day in their burrows and only come out to feed after dark. The desert tarantula, from North America, preys mainly on beetles and crickets—animals that also move around after dark.

Q A How do lizards keep cool?

In deserts, lizards often keep cool by hiding under rocks. The shovel-snouted lizard, from southwest Africa, lives among sand dunes, where it is hard to find any shade. To beat the heat, it has long legs that keep its body clear of the burning sand. It also has special heat-beating behavior—it lifts its legs in diagonal pairs, giving its feet a chance to cool down. Once those two feet are cool, it gives the other pair a turn.

More Facts

■ Desert tortoises from North America spend more than 90 percent of their lives in burrows—to escape the heat. These endangered reptiles come out mainly at night.

Desert tortoise

■ In Australia, some ants stay active in temperatures above 122° F (50° C). In this heat, a human would quickly die.

■ Camels have nostrils that they can close to protect against windblown sand.

■ To reduce contact with hot desert sand, sidewinder snakes move by throwing their bodies through the air in a series of sideways leaps.

Large poisonous fangs

Desert tarantula

Q A Which bird has built-in sunshades?

Many birds do, and almost all of them live where it's hot and dry. They include ostriches in Africa, and emus in Australia. Their "sunshades" are feathery eyelashes, which cut out the desert glare. The ground hornbill, an African bird with a bright red face, has the longest lashes.

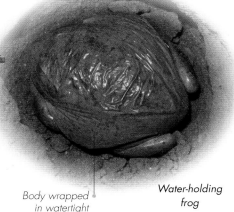

Body wrapped in watertight cocoon

Water-holding frog

Q A How do frogs survive in the desert?

Beneath the surface of many deserts, frogs lie buried, waiting for it to rain. When it does rain, the frog eats its skin cocoon and works its way to the surface. Frogs lay their eggs in puddles, and the young tadpoles soon become frogs themselves. By the time the puddles dry up, the frogs are safely back underground.

Eyelashes made of narrow feathers

Emu

Who acts as a living water tank?

Animals cannot live without water, so they need special ways of surviving dry times. Honeypot ants, from Australia and North America, do this by sipping sugary juices from plants. They then feed these juices to young worker ants, who hang upside down deep inside their nests. Gradually, the workers swell up like tiny balloons, turning into living water tanks. When the weather turns dry, the workers regurgitate small droplets of nectar for the other ants to drink.

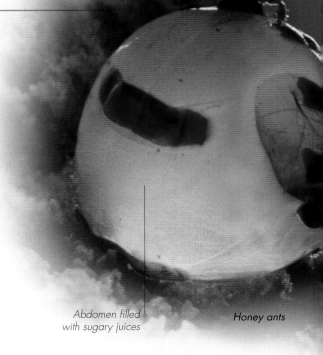

Abdomen filled with sugary juices

Honey ants

Q A How much can a thirsty camel drink?

Camels can go for a week without drinking, even in the blazing desert sun. But when they do find water, they really make the most of it. A thirsty camel can swallow 13 gals (50 liters) within a few minutes. Camels store most of this water in their body's cells. They use their humps to store food.

Water bear on plant

Water bear

Q A Can animals survive being dried out?

Some microscopic animals can survive being as dry as a crisp. One of them is the water bear—a tiny creature that lives in ponds. If a pond dries up, the water bear dries up too. It can stay like this for months or even years, until water brings it back to life.

Dromedary camel

Hump filled with fat acts as an energy store

Flexible skin

Stomach

Eight stubby legs

Water bear cross-section

More Facts

■ Aphids (greenfly) can drink more than 20 times their own weight of sugary sap in a day. They get rid of surplus water in sticky drops, called honeydew.

■ Adult African elephants need to drink up to 53 gals (200 liters) of water a day.

■ Pigeons are the only birds that swallow water like we do. All other birds fill up their mouths, and then tilt up their heads.

■ Many insects spend their entire lives without drinking a drop of water. They include flour beetles, clothes moths, and wood worms.

Flour beetle

Worker ants hang from the ceiling

Which animal never needs to drink?

All animals need water, but not all of them need to drink. Instead, some get all the water they need from their food. Kangaroo rats are experts at this way of life. They live in deserts and feed mainly on seeds. When they digest the seeds, they release water from their food, and this keeps them alive. Kangaroo rats live in burrows. They come out mainly at night when the air is cool—something that stops them from losing water by sweating.

Sandgrouse

Kangaroo rat

Who carries water through the air?

Young sandgrouse cannot fly to search for their daily drink of water. Instead, their fathers operate a special airlift. Every morning, flocks of male sandgrouse fly to distant waterholes, where they wade in up to their breasts. Once their feathers are thoroughly soaked, they fly back to their nests. Their thirsty chicks nibble at the wet feathers, and this gives them enough water to last until the next day.

Who is a fish out of water?

Most fish die if they are left out of the water. Mudskippers are different. These pop-eyed fish live in mangrove swamps, and they can stay out of the water as long as they like, provided that they keep their skins moist. Mudskippers use their front fins like legs. They breathe mainly through their skins, and they hide away in burrows when the tide comes in.

Protruding eyes give an all-around view

Mudskipper

Do penguins feel the cold?

For humans, it's hard to feel comfortable when the weather is freezing. In nature, however, some animals are specially adapted to cope with cold conditions. The emperor penguin, which lives in Antarctica, is the most cold-proof animal of all. Male emperors stay on the ice throughout the long, dark polar winters, when the temperature can drop to −94° F (−70° C). The penguins are kept warm by their feathers, and by a thick layer of body fat, called blubber. No one knows whether emperors actually feel the cold, but like other cold-proof animals, their amazing insulation keeps them alive.

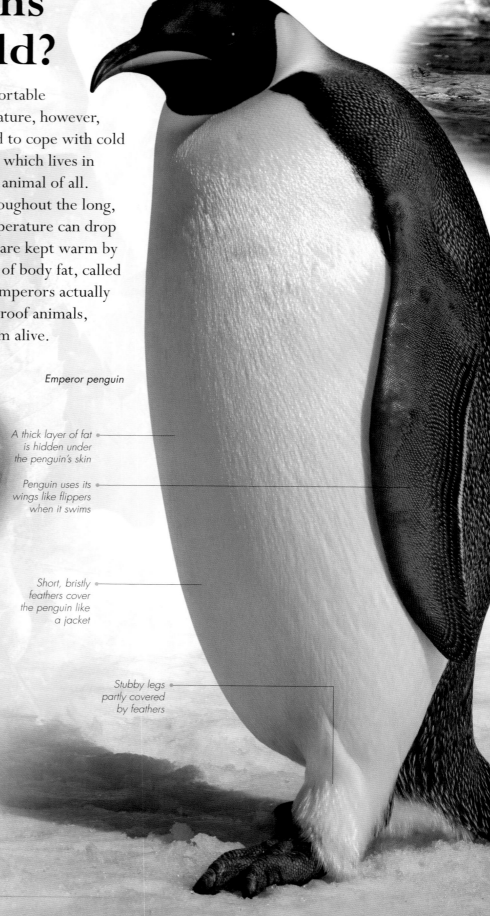

Emperor penguin

A thick layer of fat is hidden under the penguin's skin

Penguin uses its wings like flippers when it swims

Short, bristly feathers cover the penguin like a jacket

Stubby legs partly covered by feathers

Weddell seal

Q **How do seals breathe when the sea freezes?**

A Even in the middle of winter, there are seals that live and feed beneath the polar ice. A layer of body fat keeps them warm in the water, but they also need to breathe. To do this, they use their teeth to gouge holes in the ice. A seal starts its breathing holes early in winter, just as the ice starts to form. As the ice thickens, the seal works hard to keep the holes open. By the time winter ends, the holes can be nearly 7 ft (2 m) deep.

Sea otter

Which animal has the warmest fur?

Sea otters have the thickest and warmest fur in the world. Just one otter has nearly a billion hairs. These hairs are so densely packed that water cannot get between them to wet the otter's skin. This keeps a sea otter warm, and it also helps it to float. Unlike river otters, sea otters spend most of their lives in the water—floating on their backs while they sleep.

Three-month-old polar bear cubs, ready to leave their home

Polar bear cubs

Where do polar bears have their cubs?

Most bears give birth in a den, deep in a forest. Female polar bears make a different kind of home—they burrow into a bank of snow. The female gives birth in early winter, and to begin with, her two cubs are tiny and cannot see. The cubs would soon die outside, but in their burrow they are safe. Snow is a good insulator, and their mother's body heat keeps them warm.

Who enjoys getting into hot water?

Japanese macaques live in mountain forests, where winters can be long and cold. They have extra-long fur, but they also have a very unusual way of keeping warm. One group of macaques climbs into hot springs during the winter, and spends hours lazing in the warmth.

Fur changes to white in winter

Ptarmigan

Which bird has its own snowshoes?

Ptarmigans live in the far north, and spend most of their time on the ground. Instead of having bare feet, like most birds, they have a covering of feathers that work like snowshoes. The feathers help to spread a ptarmigan's weight when it walks across freshly fallen snow, and they also keep its feet warm. Ptarmigans are brown in the summer, but they turn white in the fall, to blend in with their snowy surroundings. They feed mainly on seeds, berries, and leaves.

Japanese macaques

More Facts

- Some animals—including the wood frog—can survive being frozen almost solid. Ice crystals form under the frog's skin, and its heart stops. It comes to life again when the weather thaws.

- The snow petrel feeds in the sea around Antarctica and breeds farther south than any other bird. It builds its nest among rocks.

Snow petrel with chick

- In parts of North America, garter snakes hibernate in groups to keep warm.

How do pandas survive on bamboo?

Every animal needs to eat, because food provides the energy to keep its body working. Some eat lots of different things, others are specialists, concentrating on one particular food. But for some animals, their special dietary needs can threaten their survival. The giant panda is one of the pickiest eaters of all. Although it is a bear, it feeds almost entirely on bamboo. To do this, it has paws designed for gripping bamboo stems, and a stomach that protects it from splinters as it digests the bamboo.

Pygmy shrew

Giant panda

Pandas can eat up to 90 lb (40 kg) of bamboo in a day

Panda has special wrist bone that works like a thumb to grip bamboo

More Facts

- Hyenas have such powerful digestive systems that they can break down skin, bones, teeth, and even animal hooves.

- Bloodsucking ticks can swell up more than 50 times when they have a meal. After feeding, female ticks fall off their host and lay their eggs.

- After a large meal, it can take a snake several weeks to completely digest its prey.

- A koala eats eucalyptus leaves, which provide all the water that it needs.

- A cellar spider can go for a year between meals. These spiders are common inside homes.

Cellar spider

- Some male deep-sea anglerfish never eat. Instead, they fasten themselves permanently to a female, and get food directly from her body.

Can an animal eat without a mouth?

It sounds impossible, but for tapeworms, it's quite normal. Tapeworms are parasites that live in the intestines of other animals. They are surrounded by food, which they absorb through the surface of the body. A tapeworm head has hooks and suckers that keep it in place. The largest tapeworms, which live in whales, can be 100 ft (30 m) long.

Tapeworm

• *Ring of hooks*

• *Sucker*

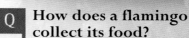

Flamingo

Does any animal eat nonstop?

Yes, the pygmy shrew has to eat around the clock. It's one of the world's smallest mammals, and it needs lots of energy to stay warm, and to keep on the move. It eats more than its own weight of food every day, ferociously attacking earthworms, beetles, and grasshoppers with its needle-sharp teeth.

Dormouse

Who puts on weight for winter?

The answer is lots of animals, including dormice, marmots, bats, and hedgehogs. These animals all spend the winter in a deep sleep called hibernation. They feed up during the fall, and then hide away before winter starts. While hibernating, they are kept alive by the food that is stored in their bodies. Marmots are the champion hibernators—they can stay asleep for up to 8 months.

How does a flamingo collect its food?

When a flamingo feeds, it holds its beak upside down in the water. Instead of catching fish, it eats microscopic plants and animals which it sieves out of the water. Its tongue works like a pump, and it collects its food with special fringes on its tongue and its beak. Flamingos usually live in shallow lakes or coasts and are the only birds to collect food in this way.

Krill

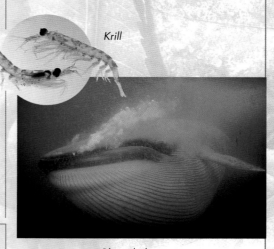

Blue whale

What happens when animals hibernate?

When animals—such as the European hedgehog—hibernate, their body temperature drops, and their heart rate slows, letting them survive without the need to eat or drink. In hot, dry parts of the world, some mammals go into a summer sleep, called estivation. Animals that estivate include some snails, frogs, tortoises, and hedgehogs.

1 European hedgehogs hibernate for up to 6 months. During their long sleep, their body temperature drops to about 39° F (4° C).

2 Desert hedgehogs can sense when it is getting hot. They find somewhere cool where they can sleep during the hot months.

Who eats the most food in a day?

The blue whale has the biggest appetite. It feeds on shrimp-sized animals called krill. A whale can eat more than 4 tons a day, engulfing vast swarms in its massive mouth. But blue whales don't eat at this rate all year. During the breeding season, they migrate to warmer waters, and often eat nothing at all.

ON THE MOVE

Which fish "flies" through the water?

Animals have proved themselves to be top athletes. Whether on land, in water, or in the air they exhibit a stunning range of skills to get them where they want to be, quickly. But few are as graceful as the manta ray as it powers through the water, flapping its fins like the wings of a giant bird. A fully grown adult ray can measure up to 23 ft (7 m) across. At birth the "pups" are just over 3 ft (1 m) wide and rolled up like tubes. They become active as soon as they have rolled out their fins.

Peregrine falcon

Flaps funnel food into the ray's mouth

Manta ray

Fins beat slowly up and down

Black mamba

Q&A Which snake can overtake a human runner?

Most snakes are slow movers, except when they bite. But the black mamba is one snake that breaks this rule. Over short distances, it has a top speed of about 11 mph (18 km/h), which is fast enough to overtake most people. Fortunately, it usually uses its speed to escape from danger, instead of for attacking. At up to 13 ft (4 m) long, the black mamba is Africa's largest poisonous snake.

How do gibbons move through trees?

Gibbons are nature's trapeze artists, with an amazing way of getting from place to place. Using their hands like hooks, they swing from branch to branch, and from tree to tree. A gibbon can cover an amazing 33 ft (10 m) in a single "swing." This way of moving is very efficient, because the gibbon's body works like a clock's pendulum swinging to and fro.

How fast can birds fly?

In level flight, ducks and geese are the world's fastest birds. But the fastest bird of all is the peregrine falcon. It attacks other birds by diving at them in midair. During its attack, a peregrine folds back its wings to make its body more streamlined, allowing it to hurtle downward at up to 125 mph (200 km/h). The peregrine slashes its victim as it speeds past.

Who is the fastest animal on six legs?

Cockroaches don't win any prizes for popularity, but they do win first place for speed. They are the fastest-running insects, and can cover 29.5 in (75 cm) in just one second. At full tilt, their back legs do all of the work, and their other legs lift clear of the ground. They use their speed to scuttle for cover if they sense danger coming their way.

Cockroach

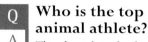
Flea

What tiny animal takes giant jumps?

For their size, fleas are the best jumpers in the animal world. They manage these giant jumps because their bodies contain special elastic pads. To jump, they squeeze these pads, and then suddenly release them, making their back legs give a tremendous kick. At the moment of launch, they accelerate faster than a space rocket.

Who is the top animal athlete?

The cheetah is the fastest land animal, but can overheat if it runs for more than 40 seconds. The second fastest is the pronghorn—a North American antelope. Pronghorns have unusually big hearts, and special blood that delivers lots of oxygen to their muscles to keep them working hard for longer.

More Facts

- Ghost crabs live on tropical beaches. They can scuttle toward their burrows at 9 mph (15 km/h), zigzagging as they go.

Ghost crab

- The world's fastest fish is the sailfish. Over a short distance, it can reach a speed of 60 mph (100 km/h)— as fast as a cheetah on land.

- Squid can power along at up to 25 mph (40 km/h). They squirt water backward through a nozzle that works like a jet engine.

- Eastern gray kangaroos can move at 40 mph (64 km/h), and jump fences taller than an adult man.

Pronghorns

1 At the beginning of a swing, the gibbon lets go of one hand.

2 The gibbon's weight causes its body to swing forward.

3 At the end of the swing, the gibbon grabs the branch with its free hand.

4 To keep moving, the gibbon starts the next swing forward.

Why do wildebeest move in groups?

In nature, animals often move in groups. Fish swim in shoals, birds fly in flocks, and antelope run in herds. Some groups contain just a few dozen animals, but herds of African wildebeest can be hundreds of thousands strong. Animals stick together because life is often safer in a crowd. When wildebeest feed, they take turns stopping and looking around, making it harder for predators to catch them by surprise. If an animal does chase them, it can become confused seeing so many animals on the move at once. Wildebeest stay together all year round, and a calf can run with the herd within an hour of being born.

Q Why do honeybees swarm?

A When bees swarm, they are looking for a new home. Each swarm contains a queen bee, some males, and tens of thousands of workers. Most of the workers stay close to the queen, but some act as scouts, searching out a good place to start a nest. In the wild, honeybees usually nest in tree holes or other covered spaces. However, beekeepers often try to catch them first. If they put a swarm into an empty hive, the bees use it as their home.

Honeybees from a hive

Males and females have curved horns

Wildebeest

More Facts

Flying ants

- Flying ants have wings for a few days in summer when they fly away to start new nests. They shed them on landing.

- Every evening, more than 20 million bats pour out of Bracken Caves in Texas. This is the largest group of mammals anywhere in the world.

- Killer whales and dolphins move in family groups called pods. The pod members recognize each other by their calls.

Q A Do lemmings really jump off cliffs?

No, they don't. Every few years lemming populations become enormous. When this happens, their food begins to run out, so they set off in search of more. Millions of lemmings swarm across the Arctic tundra and swim across streams, eating as they go. If they come to a cliff, they stop—unless nudged over by the lemmings behind them.

Incisor teeth grow continuously

Lemming

Locust swarm

Q A When do locusts swarm?

If locusts' food supply starts to run out, their behavior changes, and they gather together in huge swarms. The swarm then heads off to find better feeding somewhere else. A single swarm can contain more than 10 billion insects. When the locusts settle, they can strip every piece of greenery in sight.

Leathery front wings

Locust

Hind wings open up like fans

Powerful back legs

Red-billed queleas

Q A Which bird flies in the biggest flocks?

In Africa, flocks of red-billed queleas can contain more than 5 million birds. Queleas are about the same size as sparrows, and they live in open woodland, grassland, and fields. When a quelea flock is on the move, it seems to roll and swirl through the landscape like a cloud of smoke. Red-billed queleas eat seeds, and farmers fear them because they have big appetites. If a flock moves into farmland, the birds can devour several tons of food in a day.

Dark band around eyes allows them to look directly toward the Sun

Meerkats

Q A Who travels in a gang?

Every morning at sunrise, African meerkats come out of their burrows and set off to look for food. Meerkats live in gangs, called mobs, and stick together while on the move. From time to time, they fan out to look for insects and other small animals. If anyone gets left behind, the others notice and let it catch up. Meerkats have sharp eyes and ears, and even sharper teeth. They are known for their ability to stand on their back legs for a better view.

Do insects migrate?

Every year, millions of animals set off on regular journeys known as migrations. Generally, they travel between the places where they breed, and the places where they go to avoid cold winters, where food is easier to find. These journeys are often long and hazardous and not everyone that sets off arrives safely. Migrants include all kinds of animals, from reindeer and turtles to birds and whales. They include insects, too—particularly moths and butterflies. The clouded yellow butterfly spends the winter in North Africa, where it goes to breed. In the spring, it can fly as far north as the Arctic Circle.

Long antennae

Clouded yellow butterfly

Dartford warbler

Green turtle

Q A Do animals ever stay behind?

When it's time to migrate, most animal travelers just get up and go. But some species—such as the Dartford warbler—are divided into travelers and "stay-at-homes." The travelers live in places with cold winters. The "stay-at-homes" live in places where winters are mild enough for them to stay behind.

Reindeer

Q A Who travels the farthest on land?

The champion migrants on land are reindeer, known as caribou in North America. In Canada and western Greenland, some reindeer migrate more than 1,250 miles (2,000 km) each year. They spend the summer in the Arctic tundra, and the winter in open forests farther south.

Humpback whale

More Facts

- Swallows have amazing memories. Although they travel thousands of miles, they often fly back to exactly the same nest site that they used the year before.

Swallows

- Ruby-throated hummingbirds weigh less than a sugar lump, but can fly from North America via the Gulf of Mexico to winter in Central America.

- In Antarctic winters, limpets migrate to deep water to avoid being crushed by ice.

Q A Who travels farthest in a lifetime?

Humpbacks and gray whales can migrate up to 12,500 miles (20,000 km) a year, traveling between the cold waters where they feed and the tropical waters where they breed. Because these whales live for a long time, they clock up huge distances during the course of their lives. No one knows exactly how far, but the record may be 600,000 miles (1 million km). That's farther than a round-trip to the Moon!

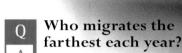

Arctic tern

Q A Who migrates the farthest each year?

Arctic terns make the longest return journey of any animal. They breed in the Arctic, and then fly south to the Antarctic to avoid the northern winter. Because they follow coasts, instead of flying in a straight line, they can cover more than 30,000 miles (50,000 km) in a single year. Albatrosses can fly for an amazing 6,000 miles (10,000 km) without ever setting foot on land.

Q A How far do turtles travel?

When turtles breed, they often migrate from their feeding grounds to the beaches where they hatched. For some green turtles, this can mean a journey of up to 2,000 miles (3,000 km) across the open sea. But even this is not a record. Some loggerhead turtles migrate between Mexico and Japan, crossing the entire Pacific Ocean. They are helped along by the current, but the journey can still take them more than a year.

Hind flippers are used to steer

Upper shell has streamlined shape

Front flippers propel the turtle forward

How do lobsters find their way?

From a single column of spiny lobsters to a huge flock of birds, animals often stick together when they migrate. Some are guided by the Sun, the Moon, and the stars, or by their own built-in compass, while others steer by "smelling" the water. Many recognize familiar landmarks, traveling along routes their ancestors have used for hundreds of years. In the Caribbean, spiny lobsters line up head-to-tail as they migrate across the seabed. The lobsters spend the summer in shallow water, but when the fall arrives they head into deeper water to avoid storms. Evidence suggests that they may be guided by a built-in compass, which picks up the earth's magnetic field.

Monarch butterfly

Q / A Do animals ever go off course?
Even the best animal travelers sometimes run into trouble. If they set off at the wrong moment, strong winds may blow them far off course. Birds from North America sometimes get blown across the ocean to Europe, and so do Monarch butterflies. Once an insect is this far off course, it has little chance of getting back on the right track.

Spiny lobsters

Q / A How do eels navigate across the sea?
European eels start life in a region of the Atlantic Ocean called the Sargasso Sea. When they are small, they set off on a voyage to Europe's coast. Their journey can take three years, and scientists are still not sure how they find their way. Some think they navigate by tasting the water, because the taste changes from one part of the ocean to another.

Young eels

Long snakelike body

Adult European eel

Do birds migrate at night?

Q **A** Birds often do travel at night, particularly if the sky is clear. The air is usually calmer after dark, which makes it easier to fly. At night, there are also fewer predators on the wing, so they have less chance of being attacked. During their night flights, birds use the stars like a compass, to help them find their way. Night-flying birds are difficult to see, but birdwatchers with binoculars can often see them as they speed in front of the Moon.

Migrating geese

Fleshy structure around nose amplifies sounds

Bat wraps wings around body when it roosts

Lesser horseshoe bat

More Facts

■ After baby turtles hatch, they scuttle straight toward the sea. They find their way by aiming toward the brightest part of the horizon.

■ Honeybees can tell each other where to find food, and how far away it is. They do this by performing special dances deep inside their hives.

■ Emperor penguins return each year to the rookery where they were born. This journey involves a walk of 30–125 miles (50–200 km) across sea ice. On arrival at the rookery the female lays one egg.

■ Ants lay a trail of scent everywhere they go. The ants then use this to find their way back to the nest.

■ Common frogs breed in the same pond year after year. They are good at remembering their surroundings, which helps them to find their way.

Common frog

How do bats know where they are going?

Q **A** Most bats have poor eyesight and cannot see where they are heading. Instead, they find their way using high-pitched bursts of sound. They listen for echoes that bounce back from solid objects and use these to find their way. This helps bats find food, as well as the tiny cracks and crevices that they use as their daytime hideaways.

Pigeon loft

How do pigeons know their way home?

Q **A** Pigeons are excellent at flying home, even if they are released far away. For centuries, people have wondered how they do it.

Pigeons seem to use several types of clues as signposts. These clues include the position of the Sun, and also variations in the earth's magnetic field. Because pigeons are fast fliers, they can get back home much faster than someone doing the same trip in a car.

INDEX

C REDITS

The publisher would like to thank the following for their kind permission to reproduce their photographs:

Key: a=above; b=below/bottom; c=center; l=left; r=right; t=top.

Alamy Images: Arco Images 52t; Troy Bartlett 37br; blickwinkel 28br; Bruce Coleman Inc 29ca, 53cb; Reinhard Dirscherl 11cr; Martin Harvey 53cr; Israel Images 49b; Eric Nathan 11br; Peter Arnold Inc. 23cl; Steve Bloom Images 50-51; Barry Turner 43br; Visual & Written SL 43r; Woodfall Wild Images 46l; Worldwide Picture Library 39bl; Ardea: Thomas Dressler 25tr, 42l, 55bc; Steve Hopkins 55tl; Andrey Zvoznikov 12bc; Bryan and Cherry Alexander Photography: 46r; Corbis: Tom Brakefield 18bl, 25cb; Tim Davis 28t; DLILLC 34l; Peter Johnson 29br; Steve Kaufman

47tr; Martin Harvey/Gallo Images 54b; Joe McDonald 37tc; Mary Ann McDonald 25tl; Juan Medina/Reuters 55cra; Reza; Webistan 59br; Jenny E. Ross 47c; Jeffrey L Rotman 27cb; The Allofs 32l; Stuart Westmorland 39tr; DK Images: Thomas Marent 8-9, 10b, 30-31, 33tr, 39tl; Courtesy of The National Birds of Prey Centre, Gloucestershire 11bl; Courtesy of the Natural History Museum, London 13bl, 17br, 53tr; Courtesy of Richmond Park 25b; Jerry Young 7t, 23t, 35br; 32l; Fred Bavendam/Minden Pictures 29tl; B. Borrell Casals 37c; Matthias Breiter 35tr; Christiana Carvalho 47bl; Flip de Nooyer/Foto Natura 16l; Michael & Patricia Fogden 18t, 35tl, 43t; Mitsuaki Iwago/Minden Pictures 45t; Frans Lanting/Minden Pictures 16br; Michio Hoshino/Minden Pictures 56tr; Tom Vezo/Minden Pictures 37cr; Norbert Wu/Minden Pictures 43c, 15cb; Natural Visions: Heather Angel 58bl; naturepl.com: Barry Bland 12br; Christophe Courteau 39br; Bruce Davidson 55cl; Tony Heald 45c; Steven David Miller 32tr; Doug Perrine 58c; Kim Taylor 27tr; OSF: Martyn Colbeck 14r; Rudie Kuiter 33tl; Photoshot/ NHPA: ANT Photo Library 23c, 43cl; Henry

Ausloos 49tr; Anthony Bannister 37tl; Bill Coster 59t; Stephen Dalton 28bl, 57tc, 58t; Robert Erwin 45bl; Bill Love 52bc; Alan Williams 56bl; Michael Reinhardt 47br; Science Photo Library: Dr John Brackenbury 13tl; Dr. Jeremy Burgess 22t; Eye of Science 23br, 49ca; Gary Meszaros 13c; Andrew Syred 12cra; SeaPics. com: Jonathan Bird 23bl; Mark Conlin 38b; David B. Fleetham 52c; Saul Gonor 19cl; Steven Kazlowski 22b; Michael S. Nolan 57cl; Doc White 49crb; Still Pictures: Fritz Polking 40-41; SuperStock: 20-21, 24b, 27b, 55tr

Endpapers: DK Images: Thomas Marent Jacket images: Front: Corbis: DLILLC; Back: DK Images: Mike Linley clb; Thomas Marent bl; naturepl.com: Christophe Courteau cla; Steve Bloom Images: tl.

All other images © Dorling Kindersley
For further information see: www.dkimages.com

Dorling Kindersley would also like to thank Hazel Beynon for proofreading and Lynn Bresler for the index.